KITTY LANGUAGE

This book is dedicated
to my favorite cats,
Mambo and Shimmy.

Lili Chin

KITTY LANGUAGE

An Illustrated Guide to Understanding Your Cat

TEN SPEED PRESS
California | New York

Contents

TREATS!

Introduction

Hello, Cat Lovers!

Shortly after my partner and I adopted our two cats, our fluffy black cat, Mambo, decided that I am his special human. Mambo rarely lets my partner—or anyone else—pet him, but he follows me everywhere, trilling to greet me, rubbing his cheek on my hand, sitting on my stuff, watching me work, and leaning against me on the couch. He also loves it when I bring out his puzzle toys and clicker and treats for games. I did not expect to get this much attention from a cat, so I joked with friends that Mambo was behaving like a dog.

I will never forget my cat behaviorist friend's peeved response: "No, he is behaving like a CAT!"

I was a new cat owner at the time (after living with a dog for thirteen years), and I had started questioning the popular belief that cats are less sociable and trainable than dogs. It seems that for every meme there is about dogs being our best friends, there is one about cats being aloof, weird, or murderous.

While it's true that, as a species, cats are solitary predators, the latest scientific evidence confirms what many of us already know from experience: cats are socially flexible creatures who get attached to their humans (like kittens to their mothers) and have their own ways of expressing affection and trust or their need for "alone time."

Behaviors expressed by other species (dogs, for instance) have very different meanings when expressed by cats.

At the time of writing this book, there isn't as much scientific data on cat body language as there is for dogs, however, there is still plenty of proven research that shows us how cats communicate. Why are my cats rubbing their faces on the corner of the wall and scratching everywhere? Do my cats want to be petted, or do they need space? Is my cat feeling confident, frightened, relaxed, or frustrated? Are my cats playing or fighting? Being able to see and interpret cat body language is the first step to making your kitties feel safe and happy in your home.

So, what should you look for? Cats signal their moods and feelings with every part of their body: their face, eyes, ears, whiskers, and tail; their changing postures; and the direction and speed of their movements. But you need to look at more than any single body part or pose to really know what a cat is saying. If a cat with an arched back and bristly tail is retreating and hissing, they're probably terrified. On the other hand, if they're bouncing and skipping sideways, they might be feeling playful.

Learning to recognize cat body language is about observing movements in context and understanding the connection between behavior and the bigger picture. Writing and illustrating this little book has opened my eyes to the ways my cats talk to each other and to me, and it has given me a new appreciation for the sensitive, intelligent, and expressive animals they—and all cats—are. I hope reading *Kitty Language* does the same for you.

Lili ×

Things to Remember

1. Look at the WHOLE BODY IN ACTION

Always look at the cat's whole body in action, even while observing changes in single body parts.

2. Look at the CONTEXT

Every behavior has a purpose, and to understand what your cat is saying and why, look at the situation in which the behavior is happening.

3. Every cat is an INDIVIDUAL

A cat's behaviors are also determined by their age, health, breed, sex, genetics, and unique past experiences. For example, a cat who was socialized with people when they were a tiny kitten might behave differently around people from a cat who didn't have these early positive experiences. It is normal for every individual cat to behave differently in similar situations.

LOOK AT
THE WHOLE BODY
IN ACTION

LOOK AT THE
CONTEXT

EVERY CAT
IS AN
INDIVIDUAL

SCENT

Even though we humans cannot interpret scent and pheromones, we can see behaviors related to scent communication in our cats.

Scent Communication

Every cat has a *signature* scent. Cats get to know each other through scent as their primary sense.

Through skin contact with cat friends, cats mix their personal signature scents to create a *communal* scent that lets them know who is in their social group and who isn't. Cats who are friends or family frequently refresh their communal scent by touching bodies, sleeping together, or grooming each other.

If one cat leaves home for a while and returns with their own scent masked by unfamiliar smells, that cat may be unrecognizable to their cat friends at home until they smell like themselves again.

Face-rub
Scent from facial glands
INVADER!
HISSS!!!
HEY, IT'S ME. I'M JUST BACK FROM THE VET!

Scent Glands

The scent glands on a cat's face and body release chemical signals—pheromones—that can be understood by other cats. Scientists are still researching the exact locations of all of these scent glands, but so far, this is what we know:

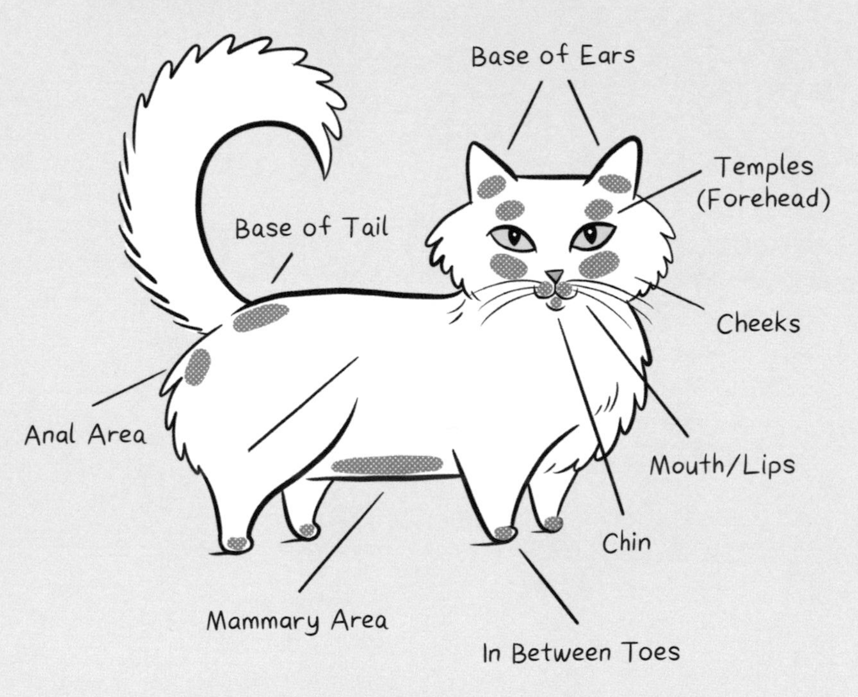

Kitty Scent Glands

Scent Marking

Scent marking is when cats transfer chemical signals (including pheromones) onto things in and around their home space. These behaviors are an essential part of how cats communicate and make themselves feel secure wherever they may be.

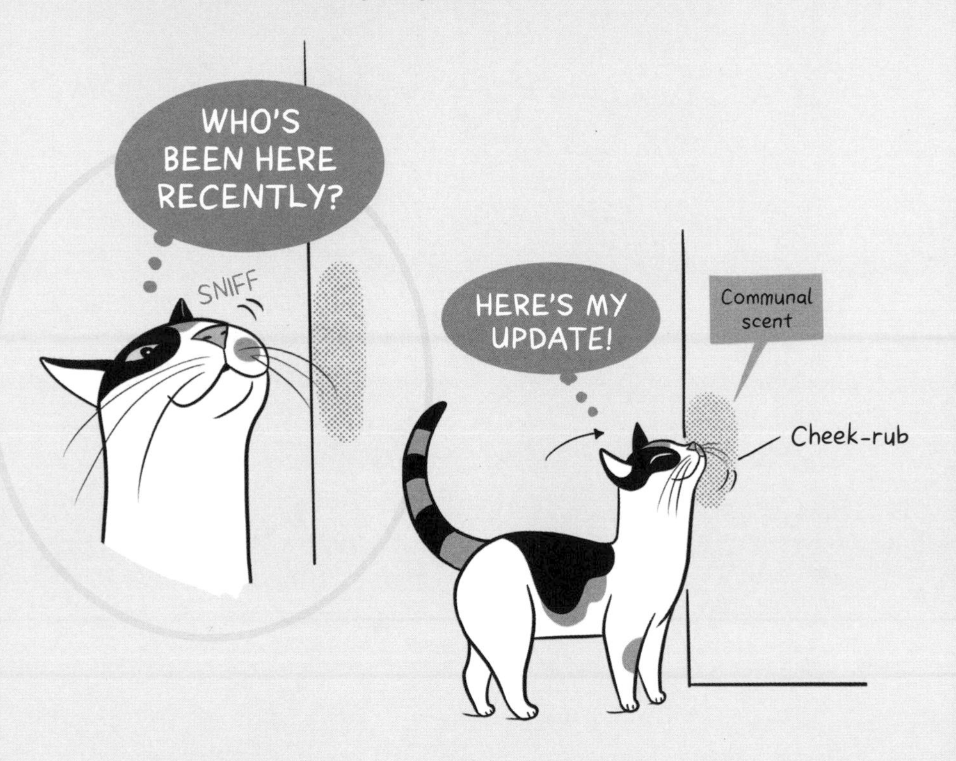

OUR HOME
Cheek-rub
Communal scent
Scent from toe glands
. . . AND CARING FOR MY CLAWS!
Scratching

Rubbing and Clawing

Behaviors cats use to transfer chemical signals from their facial glands and toe glands.

VISUAL SIGNS

- Rubbing their face and body against walls, furniture, and so on
- Using claws to knead or scratch

WHAT YOUR CAT MAY BE FEELING OR DOING

- Happy that objects and places smell familiar and reassuring
- "I've been here" or "I live here"
- Refreshing time stamps and signposts of places they have visited (the strength of a scent fades over time)
- Sharing scent messages with other cats

Toileting

The kitty toilet or litter box is one place where a cat's signature scent or the household communal scent is highly concentrated.

In fact, cats may avoid using their litter box if strong odors, such as cleaners and air fresheners, have been added to the box.

Spraying (Urine Marking)

May look like peeing, but it expresses different needs.

VISUAL SIGNS

- Tail is high and sometimes quivering (also see page 58)
- Spraying urine on a vertical surface or an object higher than ground level

WHAT YOUR CAT MAY BE FEELING OR DOING

- Stress, uncertainty
- The need to reorient and confirm where they are
- "There are weird changes in my home!"
- "I need to make this place feel like home."
- If unneutered, attracting mates through scent messages

Scent Processing (Flehmening)

Cat communication is so scent-based that a cat has two organs to smell with: their nose, and a *vomeronasal organ* (or Jacobson's organ) located above the roof of their mouth.

When a cat smells with this organ, this facial expression is called the Flehmen Response (also known as *stinkface*, *the Elvis lip*, or *chuffing*). It's often misinterpreted as angry when the cat is just processing scent.

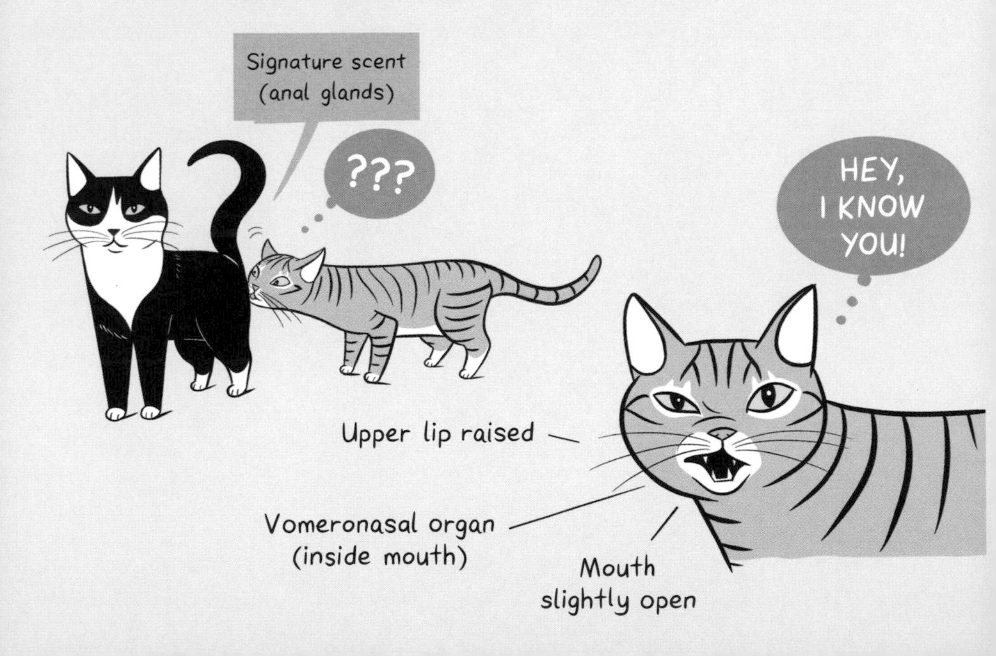

VISUAL SIGNS

- Upper lip curls up, lower lip drops open slightly
- Can look like a gape, sneer, or grimace

WHAT YOUR CAT MAY BE FEELING OR DOING

- "I'm just getting more information . . ."
- Inhaling and "tasting" a scent in high resolution
- Detecting pheromones

Note: Flehmening is not unique to cats. (Horses, rhinos, goats, deer, sheep, and dogs do it too!) The behavior looks different depending on the species.

Scent for Fun

Scent Detecting

Like dogs, cats have an excellent sense of smell and a heightened ability to track and pinpoint where an odor is coming from.

When detecting scent, cats generally move at a slower pace than dogs do, and may look disinterested (for example, pausing and staring into space) when they are busy analyzing.

The “Catnip Response”

When cats smell the chemicals from cat-attracting plants, depending on the individual, they may exhibit these common behaviors.

VISUAL SIGNS

- Rolling on the ground
- Rubbing their cheeks and chin against the plant
- Drooling, head shaking (see page 130), rippling skin (see page 129), playful grabbing, chewing, and bunny-kicking (see page 141)

WHAT YOUR CAT MAY BE FEELING

- Mellow, relaxed
- Excited, stimulated

Note: Not all cats have a response or show the same visual signs.

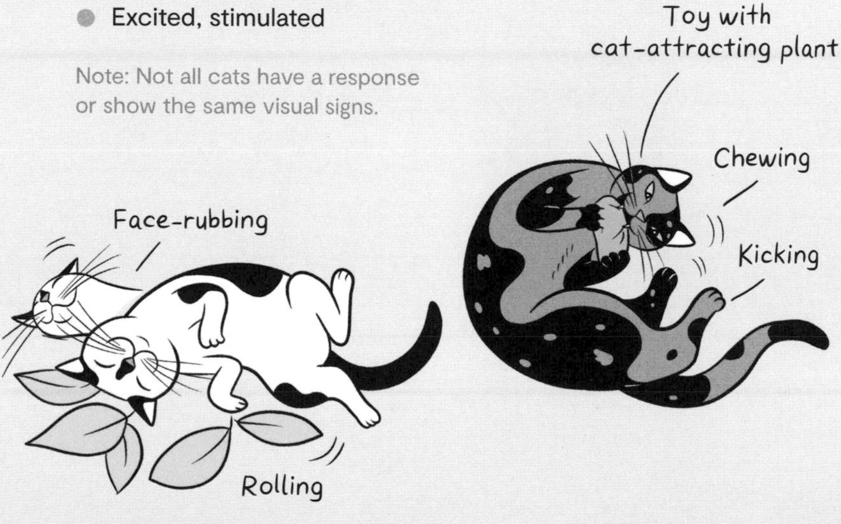

WHERE IS IT?

EARS

Cats have excellent hearing, and their ears are one of the most expressive parts of their face. Each ear has thirty-two muscles for movement in all directions.

Ears facing
forward

Forward-Facing Ears

This is a relaxed ear position for most cats.

VISUAL SIGNS

- Forward-facing ear openings
- Ear tips point upward, angled slightly to each side (the angle depends on the individual)

WHAT YOUR CAT MAY BE FEELING

- Content
- Comfortable, relaxed
- When ears are pointing straight up, alert to something in the environment

Tip: The farther the ear tips move away from each other, the less comfortable your cat is feeling.

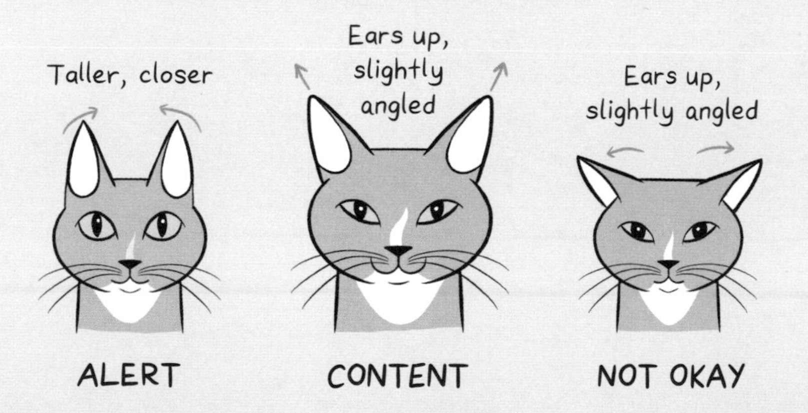

Radar Ears

Most cats' ears can move in many directions: farther apart, closer together, forward, sideways, backward, and in various combinations.

VISUAL SIGNS

- Ear openings rotate briefly in any direction, then change direction
- Each ear moves independently of the other

WHAT YOUR CAT MAY BE FEELING OR DOING

- "Is there something I should pay attention to here?"
- Analyzing the direction of different sounds
- Pinpointing the source of a sound

Looking at your cat's ear positions and movements in relation to other changes in their body language can clue you in on whether the cat is feeling unfazed, curious, or concerned.

180° range
ROOM SCAN
One ear rotates
YES, I HEAR YOU. BYE.
(resting)

Rotated Ears

Also referred to as swiveled ears, sideways ears, or *squid ears*.

VISUAL SIGNS

- Both ears stay rotated
- Tips point up or to the back (ears appear skinnier from the front)

WHAT YOUR CAT MAY BE FEELING

- Unsettled
- Confused
- Frustrated
- “Things are not okay.”
- “I need to be on my guard!”

Tip: Both ears rotated and facing outward could mean that your cat is listening to two things at the same time coming from opposite sides. You can tell if your cat is stressed by how long both ears stay in this position. The farther back the rotation, the more frustrated your cat is feeling. And if the ears are lowered at the same time, there is fear.

NOT THIS WAY
Ears rotated
WATCH IT
Ears up, rotated

Flattened ears,
aka "airplane ears"
OH
NO!
Dilated
pupils
Crouching,
head & limbs
tucked

Flattened Ears

Also described as folded-down ears, lowered ears, invisible ears, or, if the tips are pointed to the side or back like wings, *airplane ears*.

VISUAL SIGNS

- Ears appear flat, openings aren't visible
- Ear tips point down or back

WHAT YOUR CAT MAY BE FEELING

- Scared
- Anxious
- Trapped

The flatter the ears, the stronger the fear!

KNOW THE DIFFERENCE

Ears Down

In general, a cat's ears are upright and facing forward when they are feeling happy and confident. When ears change direction, look at how long they stay that way and what is going on with the whole body to know if they are stressed or not.

Stressed

When a kitty is hiding or crouching low, flattened ears let us know they are feeling overwhelmed or scared.

Just Protecting My Ears

When playing or fighting, cats may lower their ears to keep them safe. They may also move their ears out of the way when getting petted or groomed on the head.

Navigation

A kitty may lower their ears so that they can comfortably fit through a narrow space.

Stressed
Head low, crouching/ hiding
Ears flat, down
Dilated pupils
Just Protecting My Ears
Lick lick
Ears flat, back
Ears flat
Navigation
Ears flat, forward

Other Kinds of Ears

Some cat breeds have ears with limited mobility—either they can't fully rotate or flatten or they don't move at all. This is all the more reason to look at the whole body in action when trying to figure out how your cat is feeling.

ALERT
RELAXED
Very wide,
always sideways
Always
curled back
SCARED
EXCITED
Ears always
flat/folded

EYES

Cats are always watching and learning about their environment and looking at our reactions to things.

Slow blink
BACK AT YOU

Soft Gaze, Slow Blinks

A cat's soft gaze is a sign of peace.

VISUAL SIGNS

- Eye contact with almond-shaped or sleepy-looking eyes
- May include a slow, sleepy blink

WHAT YOUR CAT MAY BE FEELING OR DOING

- Comfortable
- Friendly
- Wanting to diffuse any tension
- "I feel okay with you."
- Returning a slow blink from another cat or human

Cats see movement better than details. If your cat looks like they are staring at you without blinking, it could be that they are just looking at motions in the room and not directly at you.

Hard Stare/ Stare Down

The opposite of a soft gaze, this is confrontational behavior.

VISUAL SIGNS

- Prolonged staring at another cat
- Tall posture, head held high
- Stillness

WHAT YOUR CAT MAY BE FEELING OR DOING

- Annoyed
- "This is my space."
- "Don't come any closer or else . . ."
- Preparing to chase off the other cat

Note: Staring between two cats can lead to one cat moving away or to a conflict. Look at the body language of both cats in this interaction to see what's really going on. (Also see Threatening on page 93.)

DO NOT PASS
Head held high (tall posture)
Hard stare
Stillness
I DON'T WANT TO FIGHT
Soft, blinky eyes

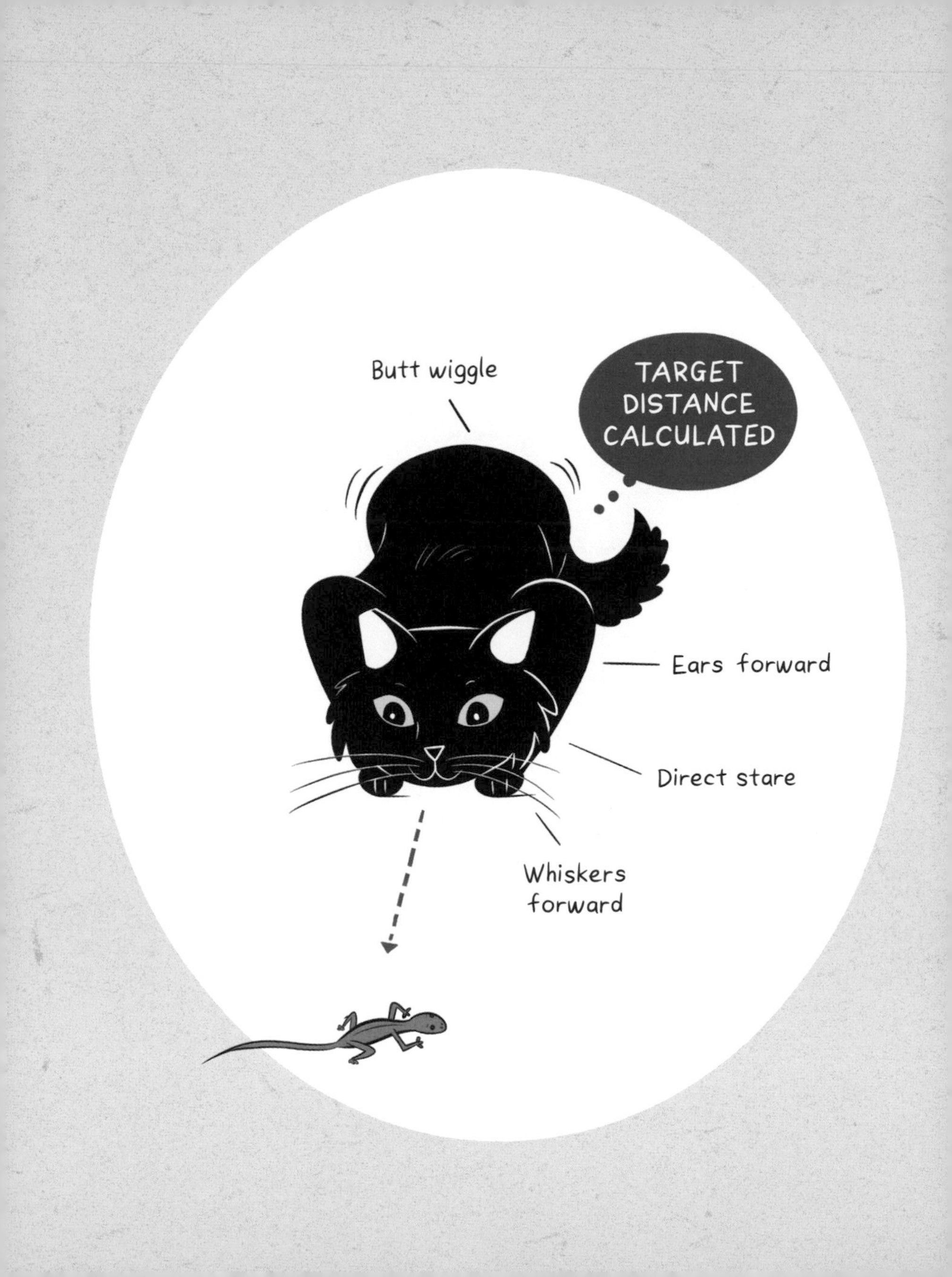
Butt wiggle
TARGET DISTANCE CALCULATED
Ears forward
Direct stare
Whiskers forward

Playful, Hunting Stare

Usually followed by an ambush move or pounce.

VISUAL SIGNS

- Intense wide-eyed stare at a small moving object or critter
- Alert ears (also see page 23)
- Stillness in the front end, movement in the back legs and tail

WHAT YOUR CAT MAY BE FEELING

- Very interested
- Fixated
- In a play-hunting mood (also see pages 139–141)
- "I'm gonna get you!"

Note: Cats have excellent vision for motion, but their eyes have difficulty focusing on things closer than 12 in. / 30 cm away. (Also see page 50.)

Pupil Sizes

As cats do not see well in brightness or total darkness, their pupils change according to the lighting conditions. A cat's normal, or neutral, pupil size may vary according to the individual cat.

Constricted Pupils

VISUAL SIGNS

- Pupils look like narrow vertical slits

WHAT YOUR CAT MAY BE FEELING OR DOING

- Needing to see better when it's too bright
- Getting a sharper focus to measure distances

In bright light . . .
IT'S SO BRIGHT!
Constricted pupils
Relaxed face & body

EXCITED
Dilated pupils
Ears up, forward
OH WOW!

Dilated Pupils

VISUAL SIGNS

- Pupils are large and round
- Pupils may also quickly dilate and return to normal size

WHAT YOUR CAT MAY BE FEELING OR DOING

- Needing to see better in low light
- Depending on other body language and the context, the cat may be very excited or very scared.

Note: Certain medications can cause pupil sizes to change.

WHISKERS

A cat's whiskers may be hard for us to see, but they have many functions.

Relaxed Mouth Whiskers

For most cats, relaxed whiskers fan out to each side and are a bit droopy. The structure of these whiskers varies by the breed of cat.

The follicles of a cat's facial whiskers have blood vessels and sensitive nerve endings to help a cat:

- Detect changes in air currents
- Measure narrow spaces to see if they would fit through
- Know to blink to protect their eyes if something is too close
- See close-up objects or prey

Whiskers also signal how cats are feeling or what they are doing.

Whiskers Spread Forward

VISUAL SIGNS

- Whiskers are spread out and away from the face (while kitty is focusing on something)
- Mouth may appear puffed out

WHAT YOUR CAT MAY BE FEELING OR DOING

- Excited
- Curious
- Measuring the distance to nearby prey or object (cats cannot see well up close)

Whiskers Pressed Backward

VISUAL SIGNS

- Whiskers are pressed back flat against the face, may look bunched together

WHAT YOUR CAT MAY BE FEELING

- Anxious
- Overwhelmed
- "Don't touch my whiskers."

A cat may also pull back their whiskers for protection, when something is too close, and to avoid them being touched. (Also see page 135 for spiked whiskers.)

TAIL

Cats rely on their tail for balance when moving around and climbing, but tail positions and movements also communicate mood.

Relaxed, high
Relaxed, low
Relaxed,
lower

Relaxed Tail

VISUAL SIGNS

- Every individual cat will carry their relaxed tail in slightly different ways when they are moving around
- Slightly curled (not stiff or tense)

WHAT YOUR CAT MAY BE FEELING

- "Just hanging out!"
- Relaxed
- Not bothered by anything in particular

Tail Up

VISUAL SIGNS

- Tail is vertical and loose
- Tip may be softly curled like a question mark or candy cane

WHAT YOUR CAT MAY BE FEELING

- Happy
- Confident
- Friendly
- “I come in peace” (and you can see my tail from far away)
- “I'd like to interact with you.”

Not to be confused with Puffed-Up Tail on pages 66–69.

Softly curled
(like a question mark)
HI
THERE
HELLO
Floppy
tip
Tail up

Quivering Tail

Seen when your cat is greeting someone (not to be confused with the quivering tail that happens before spraying; see page 15).

VISUAL SIGNS

- Tail is vertical and vibrating from the base (not flicking)

WHAT YOUR CAT MAY BE FEELING

- Happy
- Giddy
- Super excited or really wants something

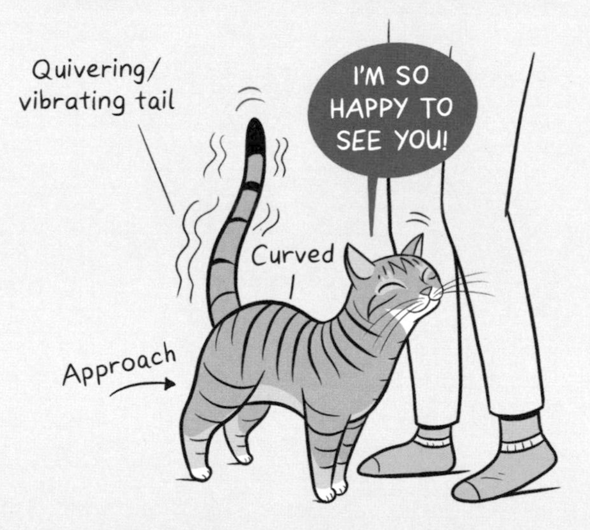

Tail Contact

VISUAL SIGNS

- Tail touching or wrapping around another cat's tail or body, or a person

WHAT YOUR CAT MAY BE FEELING

- Affectionate
- Wants interaction

Stiff tail
(lowered from
vertical)
?
Slightly
crouching
!!!
Tail pointing
down
Ears down,
rotated
Ears lower,
flatter
Tail tucked
under
More
crouching

Tense Tail

Usually seen when the cat is moving away.

VISUAL SIGNS

- Tail is held stiffly, lowered from a vertical position
- Tail tip is pointed to the ground or tucked under the body

WHAT YOUR CAT MAY BE FEELING

- Unsure
- Unsafe
- Worried
- “Do I need to get out of here?”

Tail Flips

VISUAL SIGNS

- Top half of the tail flips or swishes back and forth

WHAT YOUR CAT MAY BE FEELING OR DOING

- Engaged with the situation
- "I can't contain my excitement!"
- Busy processing something in the environment
- Fixated
- Watching or waiting for something to happen

The bigger the tail movement, the stronger the feelings.

INTERESTING!
WHOA!
Flip Flip
Twitch
Twitch

Lashing Tail

VISUAL SIGNS

- Tail is swinging or lashing—a big wagging, slapping, or thumping motion

WHAT YOUR CAT MAY BE FEELING

- Overwhelmed
- Frustrated
- "This is too much!"
- "I can't relax right now."

Big tail movements could signal excitement, irritation, or overstimulation, depending on the context.

I CAN'T TAKE MUCH MORE OF THIS
Ears rotated
Lashing tail
Body is tense

Tail puffs up
Curved back
!!!
Head low
Freeze/ crouch
Tail is still puffed up
WHAT WAS THAT?!
Head up
Body relaxes

Puffed-Up, Startled Tail

Looking at the whole movement is important to understanding the whole story.

VISUAL SIGNS

- Tail fur suddenly becomes bristly, bushy, or puffed up
- When the rest of the body relaxes, the tail remains puffed up

WHAT YOUR CAT MAY BE FEELING OR DOING

- Startled
- Blindsided
- Recovering from a scare or disturbance

Puffed-up tail
(piloerection)
Head low,
flattened ears
Tail up
FIGHT
OR RUN!
Hisss!!!
Tall posture,
arched back
Showing side
of body

Puffed-Up, Defensive Tail

Sometimes called a *bottlebrush tail* or *Christmas tree tail*.

VISUAL SIGNS

- Tail is puffed up—pointing down or up
- Head is low or tucked in
- Tension in face and body
- Turned sideways to look bigger

WHAT YOUR CAT MAY BE FEELING

- Terrified
- Trapped
- Defensive
- “Stay away! Don’t come closer!”
- “Offense is the best defense!”

Also see Terrified on page 91.

Other Kinds of Tails

As a cat's tail does not tell the whole story, it's important to look at the whole body in motion and in context, especially with cats who have short tails or no tail.

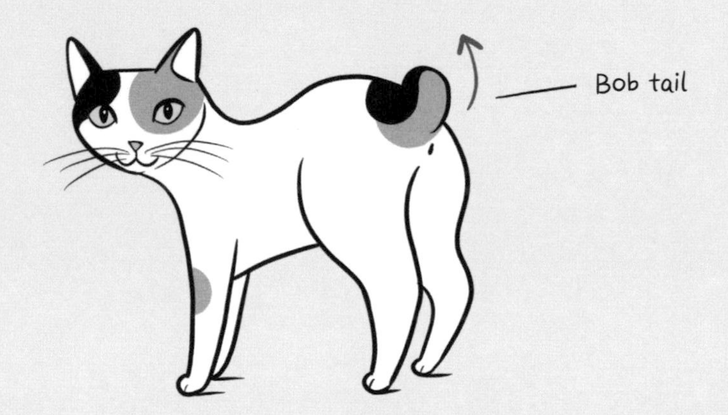

RELAXED
WARY
Crouching
Head low
Short tail
UNSURE
CONFIDENT
No tail

POSTURE

Here are some examples that take the whole body's movements into consideration.

Ears forward
Soft eyes
Head above shoulders
No tension
Ears forward
Soft eyes
Body stretched out
Paw pads touching the ground

Relaxed and Content

A relaxed cat's body looks soft and flexible and moves languidly.

VISUAL SIGNS

- No tension in face and body
- Fluid movements; not twitchy or jerky
- Weight is balanced

WHAT YOUR CAT MAY BE FEELING

- Relaxed, content
- "All is well."
- "Just hanging out!"

Tip: A cat with their paw pads not touching the ground is more relaxed than a cat whose paw pads are touching the ground.

Extra Relaxed, Comfortable

The more "open" or stretched out the cat's body is, the more relaxed and comfortable they are feeling. The cat may also be kneading with their front paws (also see Kneading on page 116).

VISUAL SIGNS

- Open body posture—floppy or stretched out
- All paws (toe beans) exposed, paws off the ground
- Relaxed face

WHAT YOUR CAT MAY BE FEELING

- Comfortable in their body and their environment
- Extra relaxed

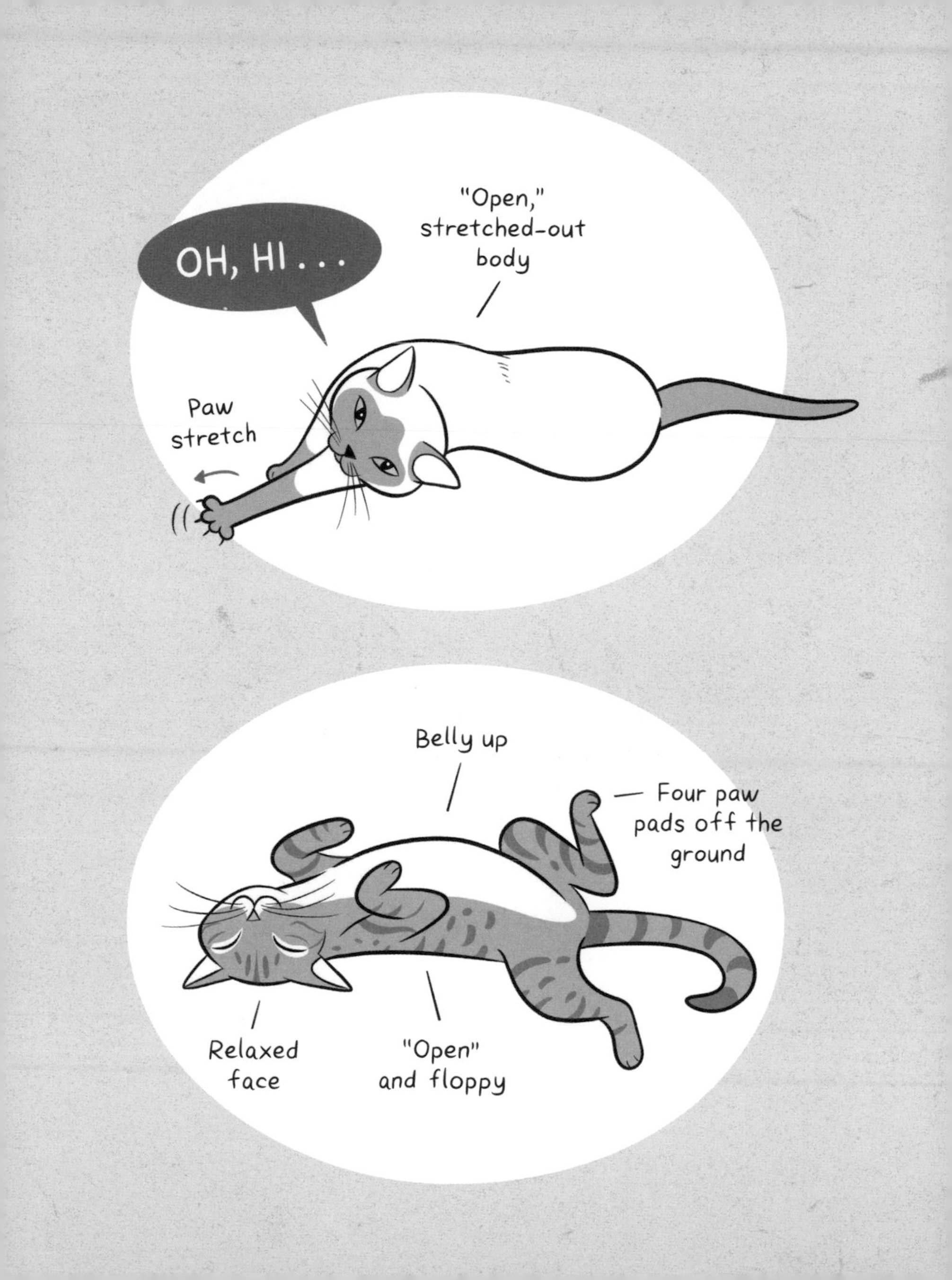
OH, HI . . .
"Open," stretched-out body
Paw stretch
Belly up
Four paw pads off the ground
Relaxed face
"Open" and floppy

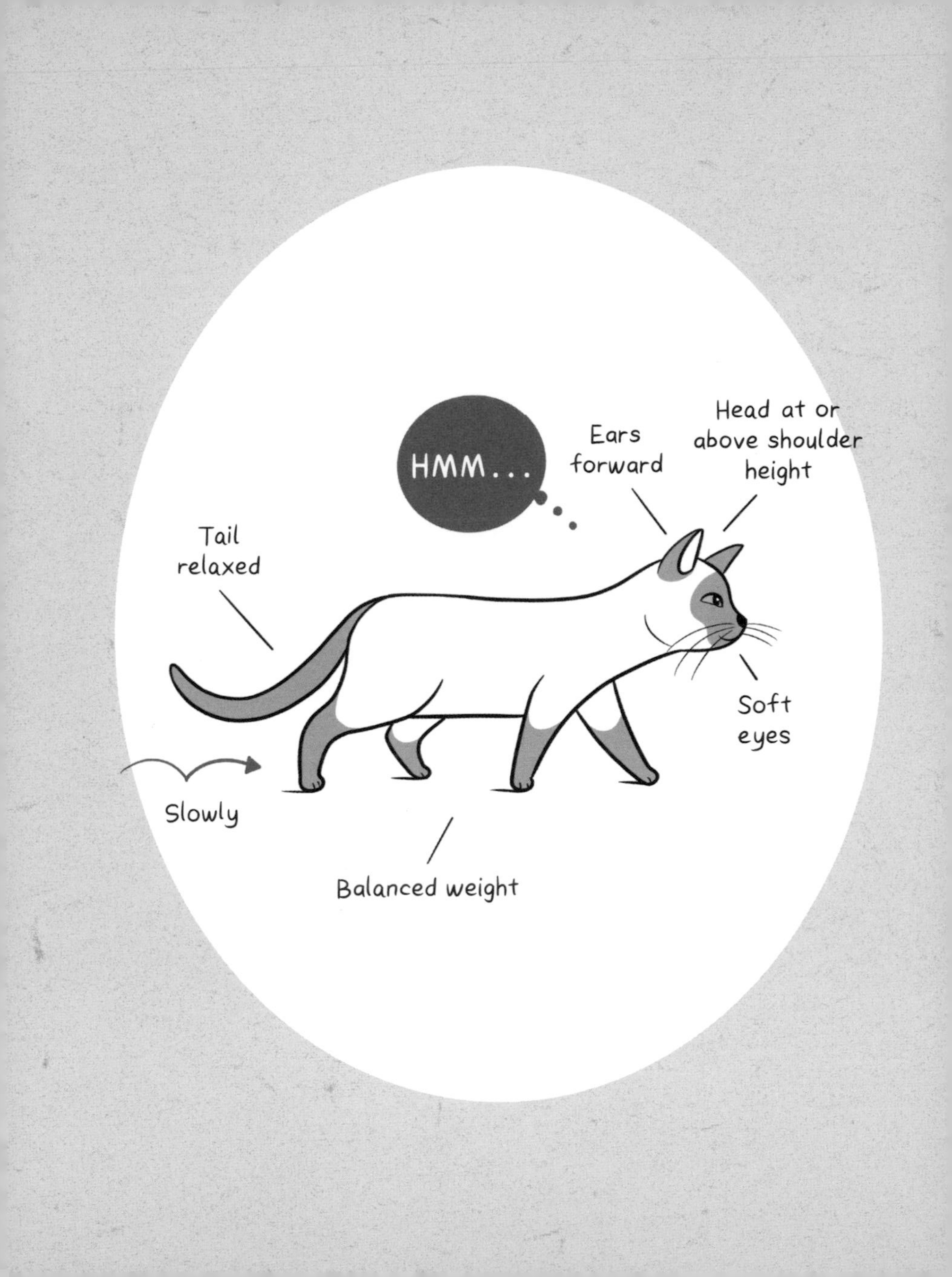
HMM...
Ears forward
Head at or above shoulder height
Tail relaxed
Soft eyes
Slowly
Balanced weight

Moving Leisurely

Relaxed cats display smooth movements from head to tail with no tension in their body. Jerky, staccato, or twitchy movements tell you that your cat may be feeling stimulated, concerned, or irritated.

VISUAL SIGNS

- Head is at shoulder height or above
- Soft eyes, ears forward
- Slow, languid walking pace
- Relaxed tail—high or low (depends on the individual cat)

WHAT YOUR CAT MAY BE FEELING

- Gently curious
- Not focused on any one thing in particular
- Comfortable in their environment

Tip: Look at your cat's head position in relation to their shoulder height. The lower their head moves below shoulder height, the more unconfident or anxious the cat is feeling.

Moving Confidently

VISUAL SIGNS

- Direct approach
- Head position at shoulder height or higher
- Ears forward
- Tail is high and softly curled (also see pages 56–57)

WHAT YOUR CAT MAY BE FEELING

- Happy
- Confident and comfortable
- Friendly

Unsure

Cats can express uncertainty in both a standing or a seated posture.

VISUAL SIGNS

- Stops moving
- Head is below shoulder height
- Slightly crouching, limbs tucked in

WHAT YOUR CAT MAY BE FEELING

- Unsure
- Cautious
- "Approach or retreat?"

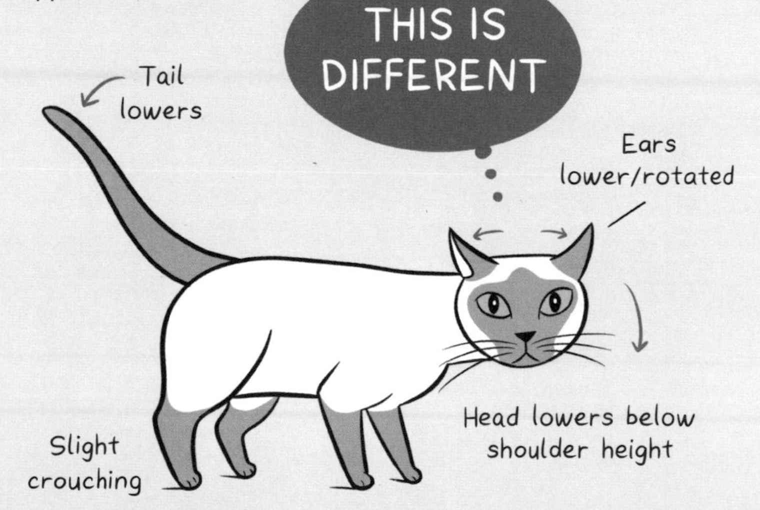

Scratch
Scratch
Claws out
THAT FEELS BETTER!
Stretch

Scratching (on a Surface)

Scratching is an essential need for cats. Even cats who have had their toes amputated (aka declawed) will attempt to scratch.

VISUAL SIGNS

- Dragging claws on a horizontal or vertical surface
- Stretched out body

WHAT YOUR CAT MAY BE FEELING OR DOING

- Happy, excited
- Seeking attention or care from their humans
- Needing to ease tension
- Nail care: Removing the dead outer sheath from their nails or sharpening their claws
- Getting a good body stretch
- Putting down pheromones (also see Scent Marking on pages 11–13)

WHAT IS IT?
Head is high
Ears up
Eyes wide
Tall

Alert, Curious

VISUAL SIGNS

- Head held high
- Ears up, eyes open wide
- May rear up on their hind legs

WHAT YOUR CAT MAY BE FEELING OR DOING

- Alert, attentive
- Slightly tense, but not enough to run away and hide
- "I need more information."

Fixated, Stalking

VISUAL SIGNS

- Body is low to the ground, neck stretches forward
- Focused stare, pupils may change size
- Waits and watches, or creeps forward slowly

WHAT YOUR CAT MAY BE FEELING OR DOING

- Very focused
- Calculating distances
- "I'm gonna get you!"

Also see Play-Hunting on pages 140–141.

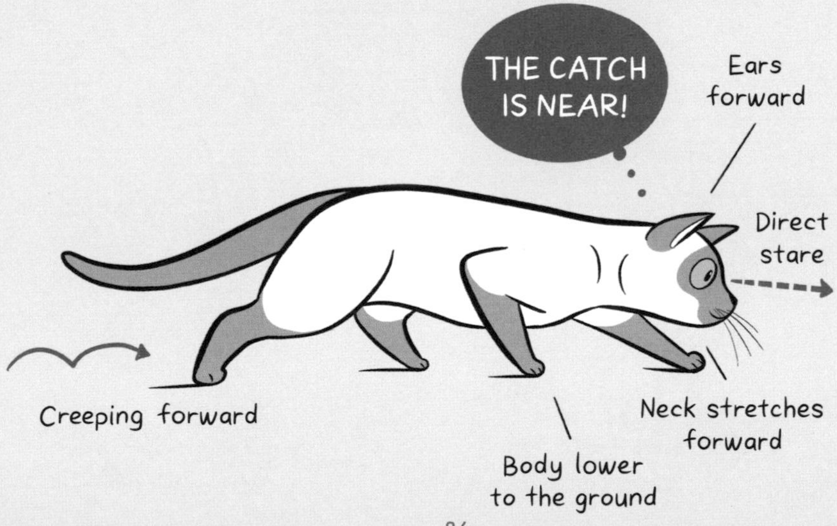

Anxious

VISUAL SIGNS

- Crouching close to the ground, keeps their distance
- Tail is low or tucked down

WHAT YOUR CAT MAY BE FEELING

- Scared
- Unsafe
- Predicting danger or discomfort
- Prepared to flee

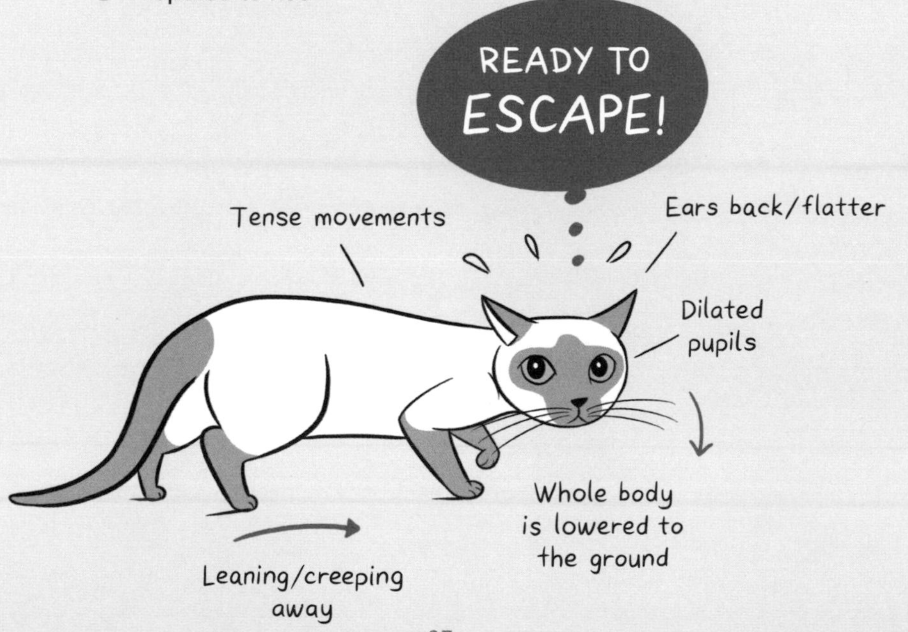

Very Scared

The more frightened a cat is feeling, the smaller or flatter they make themself.

VISUAL SIGNS

- Crouching, tucked-in head and limbs
- All four paws are flat on the ground
- Pupils are dilated

WHAT YOUR CAT MAY BE FEELING OR DOING

- Terrified
- Unsafe

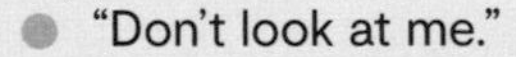

- “Don’t look at me.”
- “Leave me alone!”

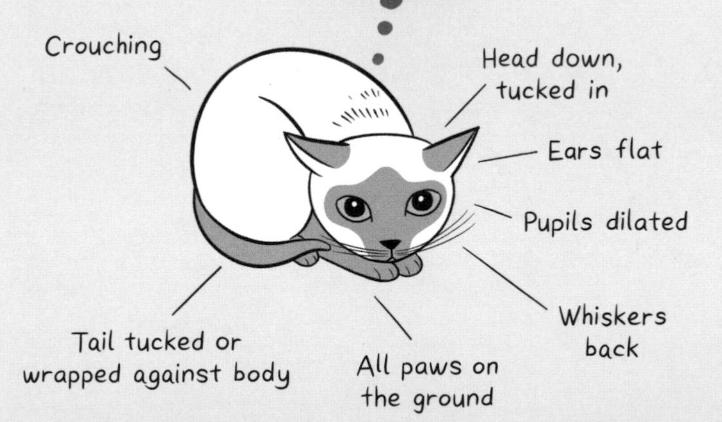

Defensive

Often misinterpreted as the cat being "mean."

VISUAL SIGNS

- Body is crouched with weight shifted away
- Paw is raised (ready to swipe)
- Ears are flattened
- May hiss, growl, or spit

WHAT YOUR CAT MAY BE FEELING

- Trapped, with no escape
- Extremely scared
- Needing the threat to go away

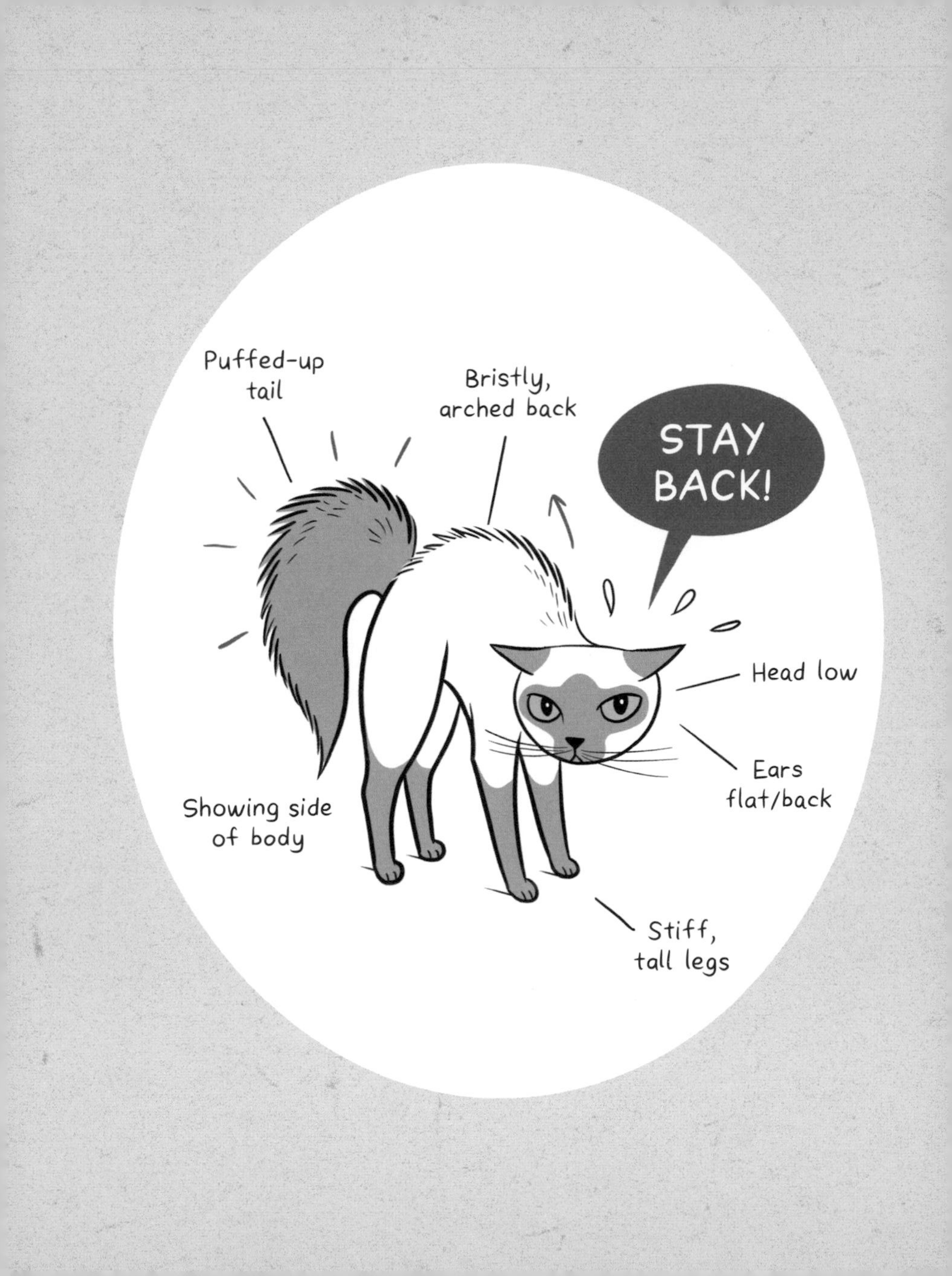
Puffed-up tail
Bristly, arched back
STAY BACK!
Head low
Ears flat/back
Showing side of body
Stiff, tall legs

Tall, Terrified

Usually known as the *Halloween Cat pose* (tail up or down), this posture is often misinterpreted as "evil" or "mean."

VISUAL SIGNS

- Standing tall and stiff with arched back
- Head is low or tucked
- Showing side of body
- Tail is puffed up—low or high
- May hiss, growl, or spit

WHAT YOUR CAT MAY BE FEELING OR DOING

- Startled or scared with nowhere to hide
- Trapped
- "Get out of here!"
- Prepared to fight back
- Looking as big as possible as a warning

Also see Arched Back on page 94.

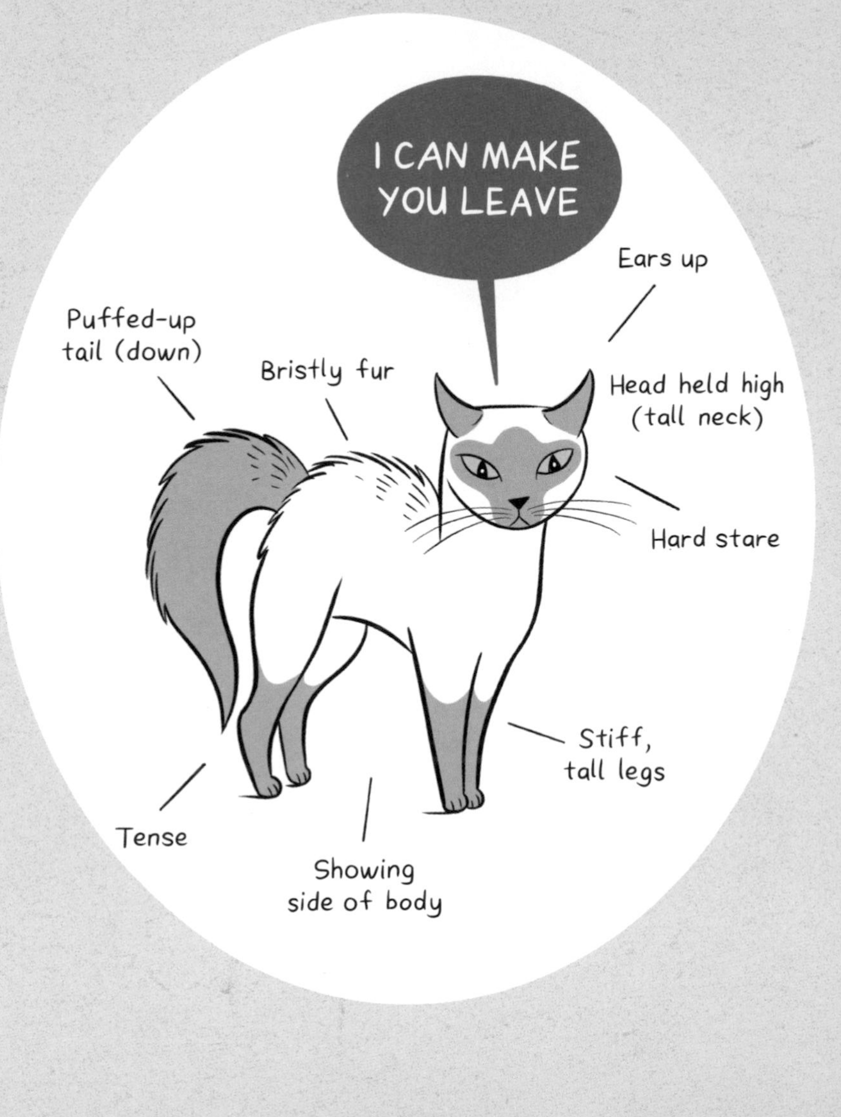
I CAN MAKE YOU LEAVE
Ears up
Puffed-up tail (down)
Bristly fur
Head held high (tall neck)
Hard stare
Stiff, tall legs
Tense
Showing side of body

Tall, Threatening

This posture is usually directed at another cat and can be in a standing or seated position.

VISUAL SIGNS

- Standing tall and stiff
- Head is held high above shoulder height
- Prolonged intense staring
- May hiss or growl

WHAT YOUR CAT MAY BE FEELING OR DOING

- Angry or annoyed
- Needing to remove the other cat from this area
- "This is mine. Get out of here!"
- Prepared to attack
- Depending on the other cat's response, this cat may fight or retreat.

Also see Hard Stare on page 38.

KNOW THE DIFFERENCE

Arched Back Posture

Similar posture, but different movements!

Removing a Threat

When feeling unsafe, kitties arch their back high up as a defensive gesture. Their head position is low and movements are tense.

"I Feel Good"

If the whole body is loose and relaxed, an arched back could be part of a big slow stretch or a friendly greeting.

Initiating Play

If a cat is making sideways bouncy movements, it could be an invitation to play.

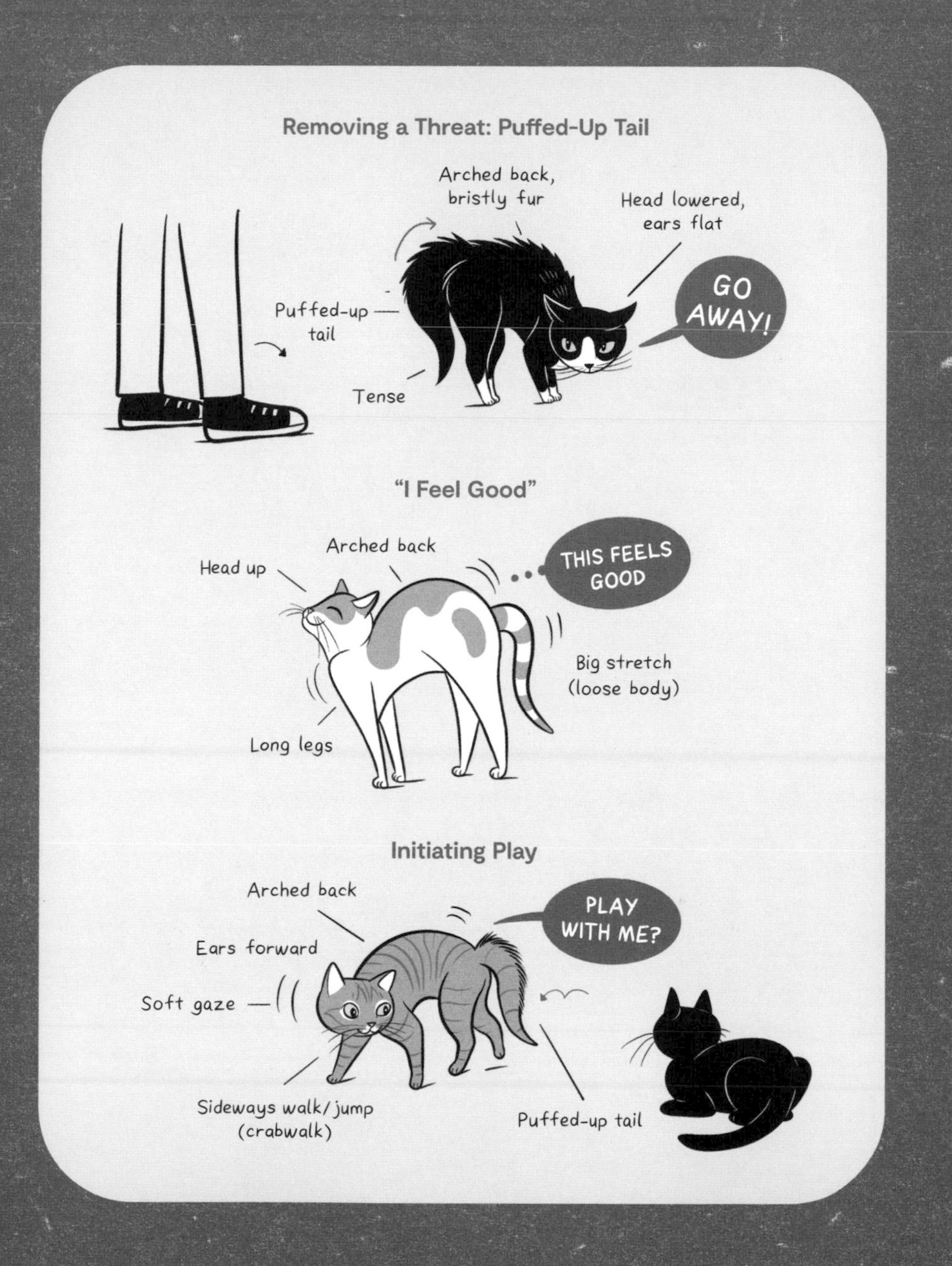

Removing a Threat: Puffed-Up Tail
Arched back, bristly fur
Head lowered, ears flat
GO AWAY!
Puffed-up tail
Tense
"I Feel Good"
Arched back
Head up
THIS FEELS GOOD
Big stretch (loose body)
Long legs
Initiating Play
Arched back
PLAY WITH ME?
Ears forward
Soft gaze
Sideways walk/jump (crabwalk)
Puffed-up tail

MEE-ACK!
MEEE-OW!
RRAAH
RRAAH!
MRRR-AOW!

SOUNDS

Domestic cats can make more than one hundred different sounds! Here are some common ones.

PRRRR . . . RRR . . . RRR . . . RRRR . . .
LIFE IS GOOD
Leaning in
PRR . . . PRR . . . PRR . . .
THINGS COULD BE BETTER
Turned away

Purring

AUDIBLE SIGNS

- A closed-mouth sound, like a rhythmic rumble

WHAT YOUR CAT MAY BE FEELING OR DOING

- Content
- Happy to be in a warm and familiar situation
- If body language is tense or restless: physically unwell, trying to self-soothe, and needing care
- Requesting something (usually a different pitch)

Trilling or Chirruping

AUDIBLE SIGNS

- A closed-mouth sound, like a short trill or chirp

WHAT YOUR CAT MAY BE FEELING OR DOING

- Happily approaching someone they know
- A mother cat calling her kittens

Chattering

VISUAL AND AUDIBLE SIGNS

- Mouth opens and closes
- Sounds like chattering or a bird's chirps or calls

WHAT YOUR CAT MAY BE FEELING OR DOING

- Excited
- Watching birds or other small prey

Meowing

Meowing is generally not how adult cats communicate with each other. Kittens meow to their mother and adult cats meow to their humans.

AUDIBLE SIGNS

- Every individual cat has their own repertoire of differently pitched meow sounds to express different requests.

WHAT YOUR CAT MAY BE FEELING OR DOING

- "Hello! Excuse me! Excuse me!"
- "Please give me . . ."
- Frustrated or distressed (usually a different pitch—see Yowling on page 105)
- Making a request for food, attention, petting, or something else

Cats reuse their particular sounds because these have an effect on their humans.

Growling, Hissing, and Spitting

VISUAL SIGNS

- Stressed body language (also see Rotated Ears on page 26, Flattened Ears on page 29, Defensive on page 89, and Terrified on page 91)

WHAT YOUR CAT MAY BE FEELING

- Startled, scared, stressed, "Get out of here!!!"
- "Stay away from me!!!" (The specific meaning will depend on the context.)

Yowling

Also referred to as *caterwauling*.

AUDIBLE SIGNS

- A long, low-pitched meow or wail

WHAT YOUR CAT MAY BE FEELING OR DOING

- Pain, boredom, or confusion
- Expressing distress in uncomfortable conditions
- Looking for humans
- An unspayed cat may yowl when in heat

FRIENDLY BEHAVIORS

Here are some common signs that your cat is feeling sociable or wants to be close to you or another cat or person.

Happy Hello!

With another cat or human.

VISUAL SIGNS

- Approaching with a vertical soft tail
- Relaxed face and body
- No tension in movements

WHAT YOUR CAT MAY BE FEELING

- Happy
- "I come in peace!"
- "Hi there!"

Rubbing Heads and Faces

Also known as *bunting*. Sometimes referred to as *head-bumping* or *head-butting*.

VISUAL SIGNS

- Rubbing the top of their head or face onto someone or something (also see page 11).

WHAT YOUR CAT MAY BE FEELING OR DOING

- Affectionate
- Enjoying the reunion
- "I like you, my friend!"
- Refreshing the communal scent

Touching Bodies

VISUAL SIGNS

- Touching bodies (in passing or while resting)
- May also touch or intertwine tails

WHAT YOUR CAT MAY BE FEELING OR DOING

- Friendly
- “I am no threat.”
- “We are family.”
- Enjoying a reunion
- Refreshing the communal scent

Touching Noses

Nose-to-nose contact usually happens between cats who are already friends. Each individual cat's body language will tell you how the interaction is going.

VISUAL SIGNS

- Touching another cat's nose with their nose

WHAT YOUR CAT MAY BE FEELING OR DOING

- Friendly
- Checking in
- Saying hello

WHAT'S UP?
Flop and roll
Relaxed face & body (fluid movements)
Relaxed tail (not twitching)

Flopping and Rolling

Also called a *social roll*. A cat may flop and roll in front of another cat to check that all is well between them and there isn't going to be any conflict.

VISUAL SIGNS

- Flopping down and rolling onto their side or back
- Relaxed face and body
- Soft, bendy movements

WHAT YOUR CAT MAY BE FEELING

- Friendly
- Trusting
- "How are you?

Sometimes used to initiate play with another cat (see Social Play on pages 142–143).

KNOW THE DIFFERENCE

Rolling Over, Belly Exposed

This vulnerable posture is often misinterpreted by humans as an invitation to touch the cat's belly. A cat who is flopped out on their back may not always be asking for social interaction.

Hello, I Like You!

When cats flop and roll over with a soft body in front of an unfamiliar person, they are feeling trusting and friendly. In front of another cat, it could be an invitation to play.

Defense Mode

If there are stress signals and body stiffness, the cat could be getting into position to defend themself with all four sets of claws.

Catnip Response

Some kitties respond to the chemicals in cat-attracting plants by rolling on the ground (also see The "Catnip Response" on page 19).

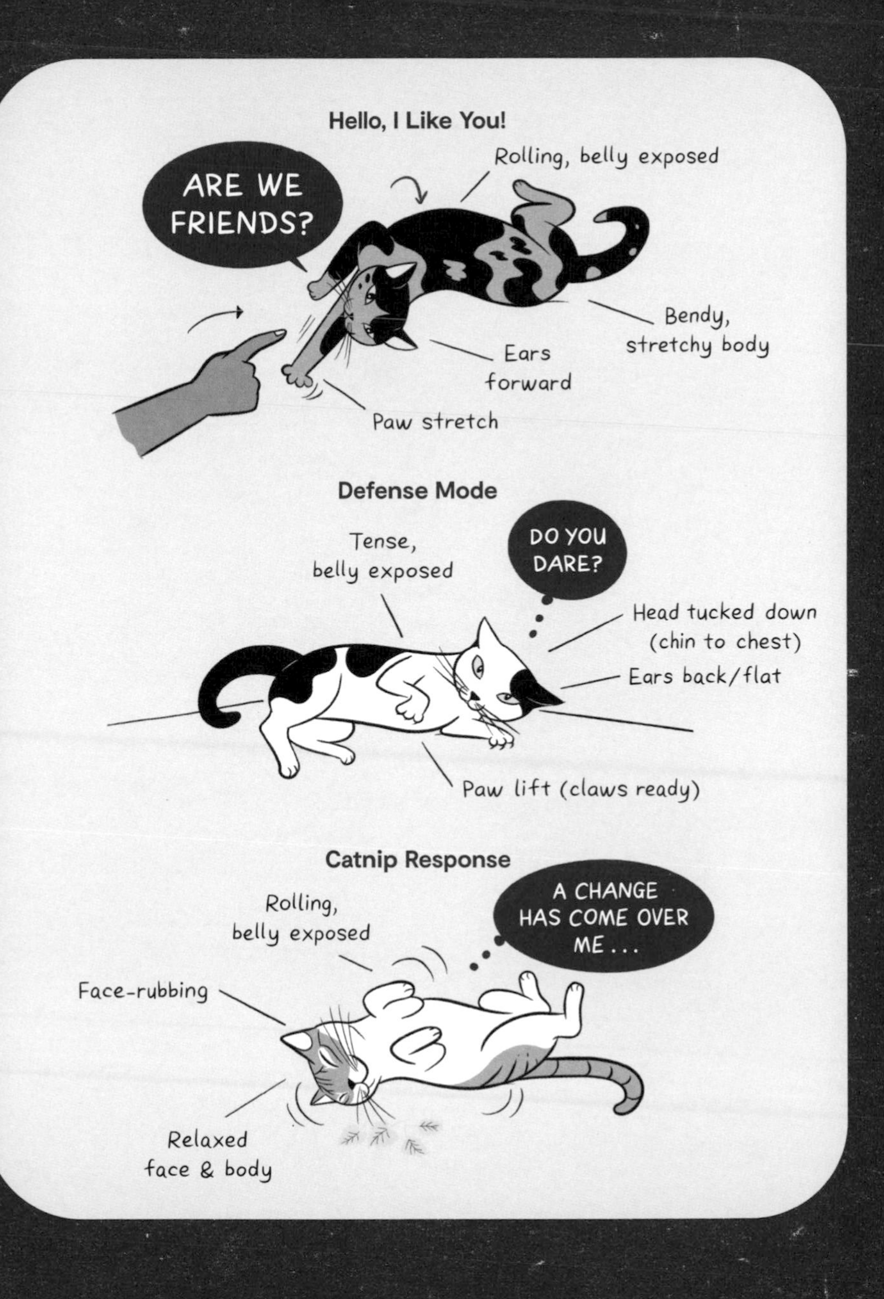

Hello, I Like You!
ARE WE FRIENDS?
Rolling, belly exposed
Bendy, stretchy body
Ears forward
Paw stretch
Defense Mode
DO YOU DARE?
Tense, belly exposed
Head tucked down (chin to chest)
Ears back/flat
Paw lift (claws ready)
Catnip Response
A CHANGE HAS COME OVER ME...
Rolling, belly exposed
Face-rubbing
Relaxed face & body

Kneading

Often referred to as *making biscuits/muffins/dough* or *smurgling*, and usually happens on top of a soft bed or human lap.

VISUAL SIGNS

- Kneading rhythmically on a surface with their two front paws
- May be purring and/or drooling

WHAT YOUR CAT MAY BE FEELING OR DOING

- Affectionate
- Trusting
- Getting comfortable
- Releasing stress
- Putting down scent from their paws (see Scent Marking on pages 11–13)

Kittens knead on their mother cats while nursing to release milk.

NICE AND SOFT
Purrrrr . . .
Claws out

Licking Each Other

Also known as *allogrooming* or *social grooming*, this is an activity shared between cat friends.

VISUAL SIGNS

- Licking a cat friend on their face or head
- May include gentle face or neck nibbling

WHAT YOUR CAT MAY BE FEELING OR DOING

- Affectionate
- Friendly
- Wanting to prevent conflict
- Enjoying a reunion

Allogrooming can also lead to irritation. For example, when one cat is licking and the other one is not into it, you may see stressed body language from the cat being licked (for example, lashing tail, swatting, and so on), which means, "That's enough. Stop now!"

Being Near

When cats hang out together in the same space at the same time without touching (or wanting to be touched), it is often misinterpreted as "aloof." Sharing space with other cats and humans is a big deal in the cat social world.

VISUAL SIGNS

- Cats sitting or resting nearby even if not physically touching
- Relaxed faces and bodies

WHAT YOUR CAT MAY BE FEELING OR DOING

- Comfortable
- Content
- "I'm with my family."
- Enjoying the communal scent

Cats who dislike each other and are forced to share space are merely tolerating each other if there is nowhere else to go. In this case, they may position themselves at specific distances and will show less relaxed body language.

CONFLICTED OR STRESSED BEHAVIORS

When your cat is feeling uneasy, unsure about what to do, or dealing with stress, you might notice these behaviors.

Look Away, Head Turn

Often misinterpreted as being aloof or antisocial.

VISUAL SIGNS

- Avoids eye contact or turns head away from source of stress
- Head may also dip down briefly, like a nod

WHAT YOUR CAT MAY BE FEELING OR DOING

- Uneasy
- "I need some space."
- Wanting to politely interrupt or end an interaction

Nose Lick

VISUAL SIGNS

- Quick lick of the lip or nose followed by swallowing (not to be confused with licking lips after eating)

WHAT YOUR CAT MAY BE FEELING

- Uneasy, concerned
- Put on the spot
- Needing to reduce tension

Stress Grooming or Scratching

Self-grooming is a normal cat activity usually done after a meal and before settling down for a nap. Stress grooming is an example of a behavior done out of the usual context due to anxiety or conflict.

VISUAL SIGNS

- Suddenly licking themselves while in the middle of doing something else
- Usually, a few quick licks on the side of the leg or body, or at base of the tail

WHAT YOUR CAT MAY BE FEELING

- Anxious
- Uncertain about the situation
- Needing to release tension
- Needing to focus on something else

Note: Prolonged grooming in one area of the body may be a sign of pain or discomfort, especially if you notice redness or bald spots.

CALM DOWN, CALM DOWN . . .

Stress Yawn

VISUAL SIGNS

- A short yawn
- Cat is not resting or sleepy

WHAT YOUR CAT MAY BE FEELING

- Anxious
- Uneasy
- Needing to release tension
- Needing to avoid conflict
- “This is intense.”

Rippling Skin

VISUAL SIGNS

- Back skin or fur ripples, rolls, or twitches when touched

WHAT YOUR CAT MAY BE FEELING

- Uncomfortable
- Irritated
- Needing to release tension

Note: Rippling skin without any touching can be caused by certain medications; cat-attracting plants; and Feline Hyperesthesia Syndrome, a medical condition in which a cat's skin has extreme sensitivity and rippling when touched.

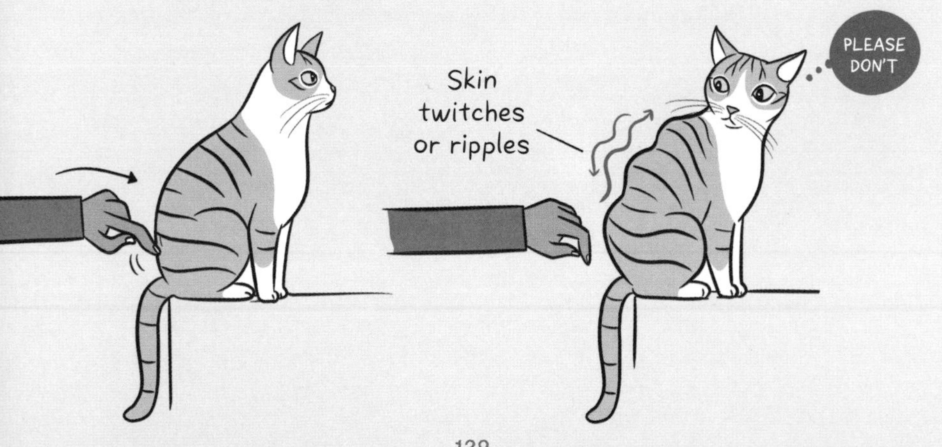

Shake-Off

VISUAL SIGNS

- Head or body shake-off (when not wet)

WHAT YOUR CAT MAY BE FEELING OR DOING

- "Enough, thank you!"
- Stress release
- Releasing tension after an intense experience (positive or negative)

Note: Frequent head shaking can also be a sign of an ear infection.

Hiding

VISUAL SIGNS

- Staying out of sight, not responding
- If there is nowhere to hide, pressing their face and body into a tight corner

WHAT YOUR CAT MAY BE FEELING

- Stressed
- Unsafe or unwell

Note: Not having a safe and private space to hide is more stressful for a cat than hiding.

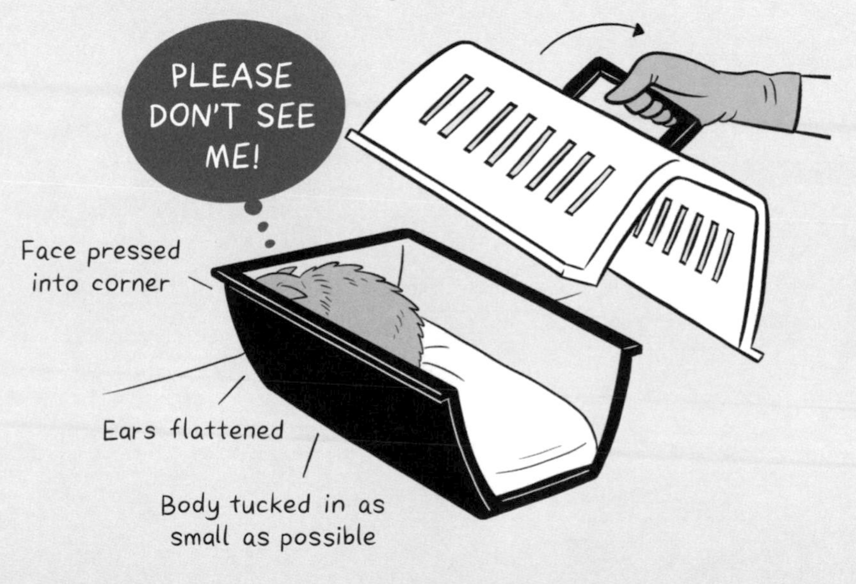

Zoomies

Zoomies are a normal way to release stress.

VISUAL SIGNS

- Suddenly running around really fast, almost bouncing off the walls
- May include jumping, climbing, pouncing, meowing, scratching, and biting

WHAT YOUR CAT MAY BE FEELING

- Pressure release
- Relief
- A release of pent-up energy following a long period of sleeping or boredom
- Overstimulated

Cats usually launch into zoomies at the start of their natural waking hours (dusk and dawn), and also after pooping.

Mrrriaow!!!
AT LAST!!!

Pretending to Sleep

A cat may pretend to be asleep if there is nowhere safe to hide.

VISUAL SIGNS

- Huddled, crouching posture, not responding
- Head is tucked into body
- Eyes are not fully shut

WHAT YOUR CAT MAY BE FEELING

- Very stressed
- Shut down
- "If I look like I am asleep, they may leave me alone."

"Pain Face"

VISUAL SIGNS

- Head is tucked down toward the chest
- Ear tips are far apart
- Eyes are squinting, avoiding eye contact
- Whiskers are straighter, spikier than normal
- Corners of mouth are stretched backward

WHAT YOUR CAT MAY BE FEELING

- Some degree of pain

Note: Neutral ear and whisker positions will vary according to the individual cat.

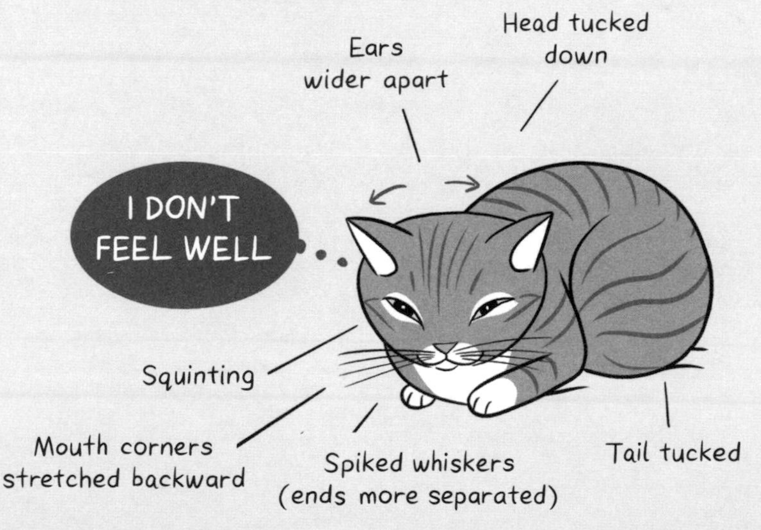

PLAY

In the cat world, there are two main ways to play: play-hunting (with small objects and prey) and social play (with cat friends).

Chase
Pounce
Scoop-toss
Grab

Play-Hunting

Also known as *predatory play*, *prey play*, and *object play*.

Hunting behaviors are essential to a cat's health and a key part of being a cat. Cats are solitary hunters, so play-hunting is a solo activity done with small objects, including toys made to move like prey by a human hand. Play-hunting is lots of fun for a cat and also a great way for you to bond with your cat and learn what they like. When cats play-hunt, they use their claws and teeth to interact with the prey.

As a cat matures, they may spend less time doing "tooth and claw" and enjoy more "stalk and ambush" activity.

Watch and wait . . .

Ambush mode

Stalk and Ambush

- Intense focus on object that moves like prey
- Preparing to pounce

Tooth and Claw

- Scooping and tossing
- Swatting, grabbing, and holding . . .
- Raking (bunny-kicking) with their back paws
- Biting to kill

Ears forward, tail up
Flop!
GAME ON?
Soft eyes
Stare-off

Social Play

Cat play is easily misinterpreted as fighting. When two cats are playing, it is non-serious "ritualized conflict." Their rough and tumble play body language can look like aggression, but it's more like a sporting event.

VISUAL SIGNS

- Stare-offs
- Rotating ears
- Arched backs and puffed-up fur
- Big tail movements

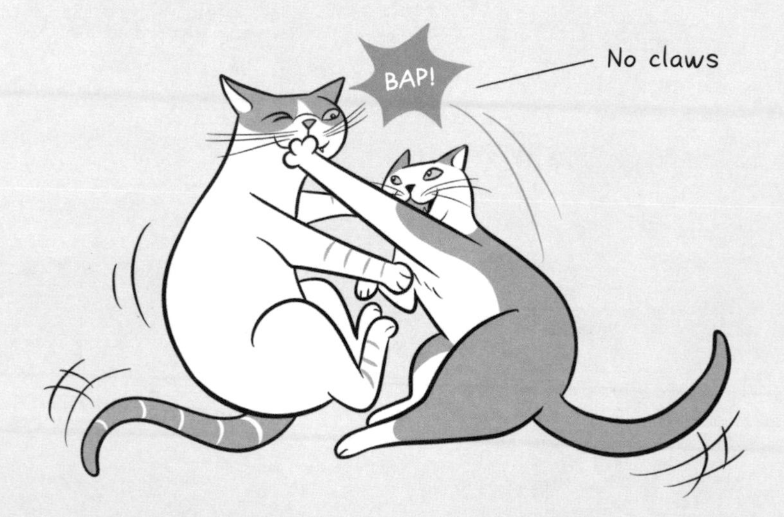

How We Know This Is Fun Play

- Mostly silent (no hissing, growling, or squealing)
- Swatting or smacking with claws in—no pain or injury
- Biting is inhibited—no pain or injury
- Cats swap top and bottom positions
- Lots of short pauses (also see Play Pauses on page 146)
- Easy for either cat to leave, but they choose to return or stick around

In the context of play these are all non-threatening signs, and both cats stick around for the action until one cat leaves. Claws and teeth are kept in check and not used to hurt or kill. Usually, both cats have a friendly relationship and allogroom (see pages 118–119).

Play Pauses

Cats are easily distracted, and frequent pauses during play tell you that neither cat is feeling seriously threatened by their partner.

VISUAL SIGNS

- Briefly looks at something else
- Briefly licks or scratches self
- Brief head turns or nods
- Short pauses, soft blinky eyes

WHAT YOUR CAT MAY BE FEELING OR DOING

- "How can I better position myself to win this match?"
- Distracted by something else
- Needing a short break
- Reassessing, considering their next move

ONE SEC . . .
Head turn
HMM . . .
WHAT'S OVER
THERE?

When It's Not Fun

Sometimes friendly play can get too intense and turn into conflict. It is also no longer mutually fun if one cat is in play-hunting mode and the other cat is being hunted.

Pay attention to the body language and movements of each individual cat to know if this is mutually fun play, fun for only one cat, or an actual fight.

How We Know It's a Fight or Not Mutually Fun

VISUAL AND AUDITORY SIGNS

- Hissing, growling, or shrieking sounds
- Intense interaction with no pauses (prolonged stare-off, stress signals)
- Pain or injury from biting and swatting
- One cat is pursuing, while the other cat tries to escape or leaves and doesn't come back
- In a true fight between two cats, nobody is able to easily leave.

KNOW THE DIFFERENCE

Swat

A cuff, swat, or paw slap is often misinterpreted as an "aggressive" or "jerk" move because sometimes claws are involved. To know what's really going on, pay attention to what happens before and after the action.

Play-Hunting Activated!

If swatting something makes it move so you want to swat it again . . . this kitty is having fun.

Stop Doing That

If smaller communication signals have had no effect, kitties may use their paw to prevent further torment. "That's enough, thank you."

Extra Benefits

If a kitty is feeling curious about an object, they may investigate with their paw. Sometimes, there are big rewards, like getting extra attention from your human.

Play-Hunting Activated!
SO MUCH FUN
Stop Doing That
I said STOP IT
Extra Benefits
OOOPS! DO I HAVE YOUR ATTENTION?

Congratulations

You have now taken the first steps in understanding your cat's body language.

For more resources on cat behavior, please visit kittylanguagebook.com.

THANK YOU

My deepest gratitude to the following cat behavior consultants and scientists for helping me with this book.

- Caroline Crevier-Chabot
- Dr. Mikel Delgado
- Sarah Dugger
- Dr. Sarah Ellis
- Hanna Fushihara
- Dr. Emma K. Grigg
- Rochelle Guardado
- Julia Henning
- Jacqueline Munera
- Dr. Wailani Sung
- Dr. Zazie Todd
- Dr. Andrea Y. Tu
- Melinda Trueblood-Stimpson
- Dr. Kristyn Vitale

Thank you also to: The amazing team at Ten Speed Press—Julie Bennett, Isabelle Gioffredi, Terry Deal, and Dan Myers—for making this book beautiful.

My agent, Lilly Ghahremani, who always has my back.

Friends and family for their support and for reading through early drafts: Nathan Long, Linda Lombardi, Solvej Schou, Kitty Scott, Alice Tong, Kiem Sie, Ta-Te Wu, Christa Faust, and Dr. Eduardo J. Fernandez.

Published in the United States by
Ten Speed Press, an imprint of
Random House, a division of Penguin
Random House LLC, New York.
TenSpeed.com
RandomHouseBooks.com

Typefaces: TIGHTYPE's Moderat
and Nicky Laatz's Fandango

Library of Congress Cataloging-in-
Publication Data
Names: Chin, Lili, author.
Title: Kitty language : an illustrated
guide to understanding your cat
/ Lili Chin.
Description: First edition. | New York
: Ten Speed Press, an imprint
of Random House, a division of
Penguin Random House LLC, [2023]
Identifiers: LCCN 2022042554 (print)
| LCCN 2022042555 (ebook)
| ISBN 9781984861986 (hardcover)
| ISBN 9781984861993 (ebook)
Subjects: LCSH: Cats—Behavior.
Classification: LCC SF446.5 .C47
2023 (print) | LCC SF446.5 (ebook)
| DDC 636.8—dc23/eng/20221115
LC record available at https://lccn
.loc.gov/2022042554
LC ebook record available at
https://lccn.loc.gov/2022042555

Hardcover ISBN: 978-1-9848-6198-6
eBook ISBN: 978-1-9848-6199-3

Printed in China

Editor: Julie Bennett
Production editor: Terry Deal
Designer: Isabelle Gioffredi
Production designer: Claudia Sanchez
Production manager: Dan Myers
Copyeditor: Surina Jain
Proofreader: Marlene Tungseth
Publicist: Natalie Yera
Marketer: Brianne Sperber

10 9 8 7 6 5 4 3 2

First Edition